THE PARABLES

The Unmerciful Servant

Matthew 18:21-35

RETOLD BY MARY BERENDES • ILLUSTRATED BY ROBERT SQUIER

Distributed by The Child's World®
1980 Lookout Drive • Mankato, MN 56003-1705
800-599-READ • www.childsworld.com

ACKNOWLEDGMENTS
The Child's World®: Mary Berendes, Publishing Director
The Design Lab: Art Direction and Design
Red Line Editorial: Contributing Editor
Natalie Mortensen: Contributing Editor

LIBRARY OF CONGRESS CATALOGING-IN-PUBLICATION DATA
Berendes, Mary.
 The unmerciful servant / by Mary Berendes; illustrated by Robert Squier.
   p. cm.
 ISBN 978-1-60954-396-9 (library reinforced: alk. paper)
 1. Unforgiving servant (Parable)—Juvenile literature. I. Squier, Robert. II. Title.
 BT378.U37B47 2011
 226.8'09505—dc22   2011004996

Printed in the United States of America in Mankato, Minnesota.
July 2011
PA02087

The parables of the Bible are simple, easy-to-remember stories that Jesus told. Even though the stories are simple, they have deeper meanings.

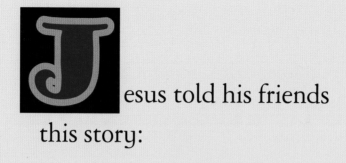

esus told his friends
this story:

———◆———

There once was a rich king.
The king's servants owed
him money.

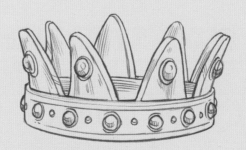

The king decided to
have his servants settle
their accounts. Many of the
servants quickly paid their
debts. But one servant owed
one thousand coins.

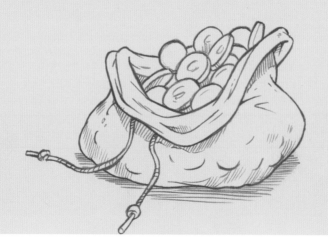

The servant could not pay, and the king became angry. The king ordered that the servant and his family were to be sold!

The servant fell to his knees and cried. "Please, great king. Have patience! I will pay you everything," he begged.

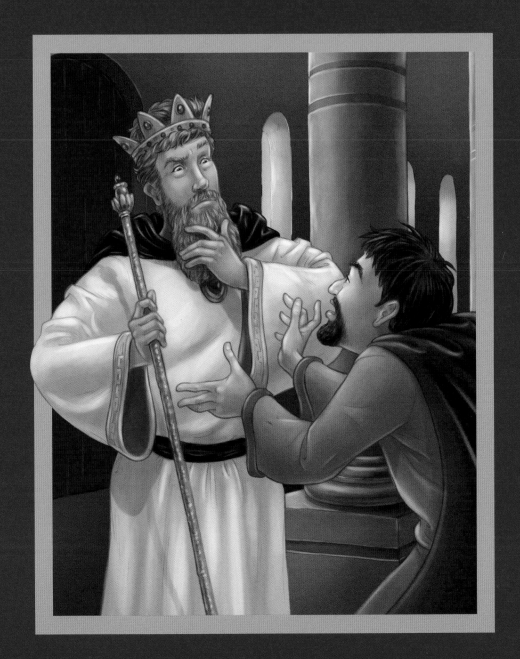

The king felt sorry for the servant. He decided to be patient and let the servant slowly pay off his debt.

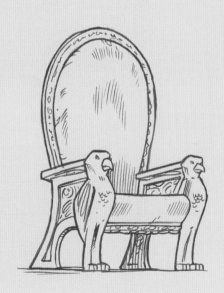

The servant thanked the king and left the room. As he passed the gate, he saw a man that owed him money. The servant grabbed the man and shook him. "Pay me what you owe!" he yelled.

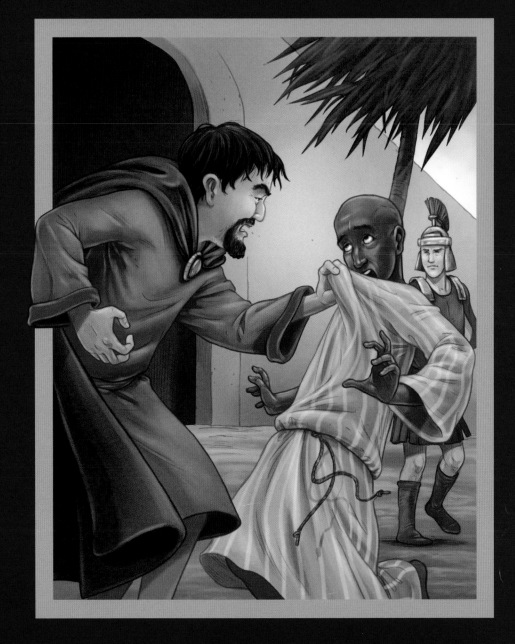

The man could not pay his debt to the servant. "Please, have patience!" the man cried. But the servant was not patient. He had the man thrown in jail.

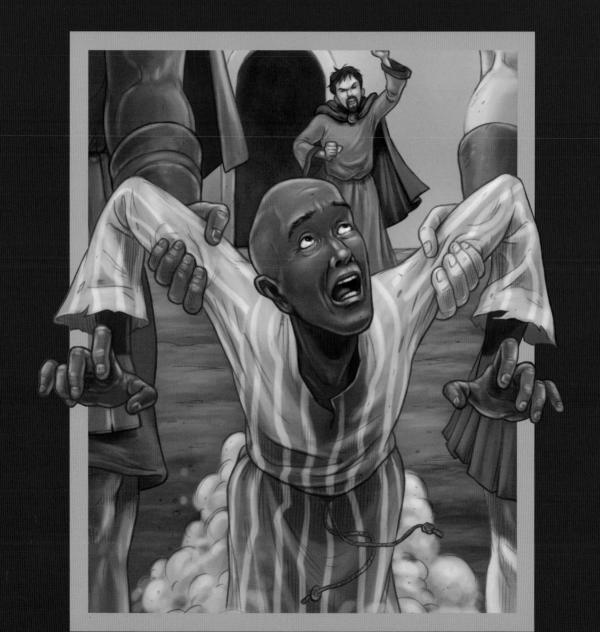

The king soon heard what had happened. He called the servant before him and said, "You wicked servant! I forgave you and showed you patience. Yet you did not do the same to others! I shall now throw you in jail until you can pay your debt to me."

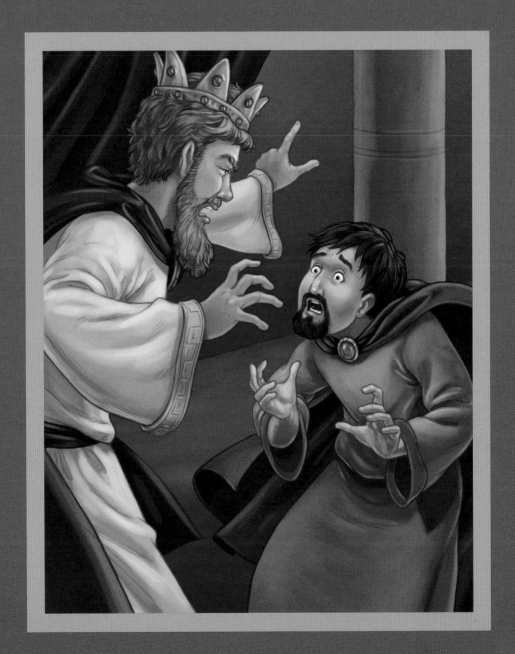

"There is a lesson to this story," said Jesus. "Remember, God has forgiven you much, so you should forgive others much."

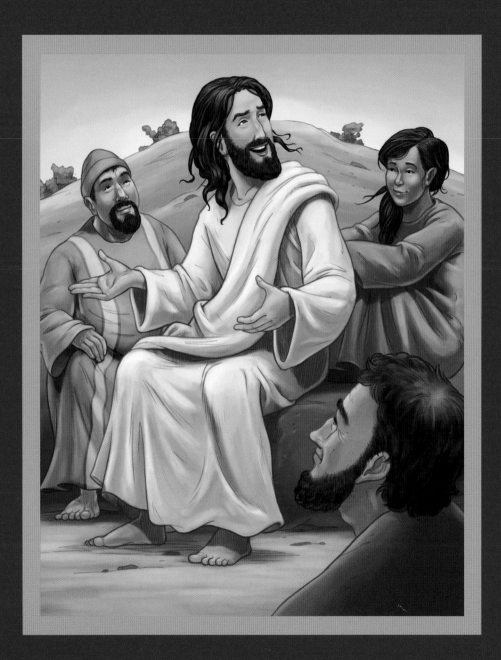

BEYOND THE STORY

Jesus often preached about the power of forgiveness. His disciples once asked him how many times they must forgive a brother when he sinned against them. Jesus answered that their forgiveness should be unlimited. Jesus is telling us that there is no limit to the number of times you can be forgiven. Since God forgives our sins, we should also forgive those people who offend us.

The parable of the unmerciful servant helps show what happens if we choose not to forgive. Jesus illustrates his point by telling the story of the rich king and his servants. The king represents God, our father. Like a king, he protects us and takes care of us. He also expects us to follow his rules and live good lives.

The servants are examples of God's children. In the parable, the king forgives the debt of his servant. By showing his mercy, the king hopes that his servant will go forward and do the same to others. The servant, however, does not practice forgiveness. This makes the king sad and angry. The king punishes the servant for not learning the lesson of forgiveness. The unmerciful servant's refusal to show the same mercy to the man who owed him money shows that he did not really appreciate his own forgiveness. Like God, the king's punishment was an effort to show his servant the importance of forgiveness and to help teach him to appreciate his own.

Jesus is telling us that there is no limit to the forgiveness that God will show us for our sins. By not placing a limit on the number of times that you will forgive, you are showing mercy toward others. When you live your life this way, it is a reflection of a good relationship with God.

Mary Berendes has authored dozens of books for children, including nature titles as well as books about countries and holidays. She loves to collect antique books and has some that are almost 200 years old. Mary lives in Minnesota.

Robert Squier has been drawing ever since he could hold a crayon. Today, instead of using crayons, he uses pencils, paint, and the computer. Robert lives in New Hampshire with his wife.